Portland Maine
Soldiers
and
Sailors

A Brief Sketch
of the
Part They Took in the
War of the Rebellion

B. Thurston and Co.

HERITAGE BOOKS
2011

HERITAGE BOOKS
AN IMPRINT OF HERITAGE BOOKS, INC.

Books, CDs, and more—Worldwide

For our listing of thousands of titles see our website
at
www.HeritageBooks.com

A Facsimile Reprint
Published 2011 by
HERITAGE BOOKS, INC.
Publishing Division
100 Railroad Ave. #104
Westminster, Maryland 21157

Originally published in Portland:
Printed by B. Thurston & Co.
1884

— Publisher's Notice —

In reprints such as this, it is often not possible to remove blemishes from the original. We feel the contents of this book warrant its reissue despite these blemishes and hope you will agree and read it with pleasure.

International Standard Book Numbers
Paperbound: 978-0-7884-3025-1
Clothbound: 978-0-7884-8783-5

Portland Soldiers and Sailors.

Mr. Sylvester B. Beckett, who is the only one, so far as we know, that ever attempted to learn how many soldiers and sailors went into the army or navy from Portland during the rebellion, states the number to have been "about five thousand."*

The population in 1860 was 26,342, and in 1865, 30,124, of whom 13,964 were males. It is incredible that 5,000 able-bodied men could have been enlisted from so small a population. Mr. Beckett probably counted the number of Portland men named in the Adjutant-General's report, where any man, who served in two companies, shows twice. This "repeating" happened to a large proportion of our soldiers; for instance, more than a half of the men of the 1st Maine, re-enlisted, and are shown again elsewhere. The consolidation of the 5th, 6th and 7th regiments, and of the 1st D. C. cavalry with the 1st Maine cavalry, necessitated the enrolling of the same names twice.

Portland also was credited with many men who came here from the British Provinces. We shall not try to correct Mr. Beckett's figures, and nothing more will be attempted in this sketch than to give the prominent facts relating to the troops from Portland, in the war of the rebellion, including the regiments which "rendezvoused" in our city.†

*See Portland Directory for 1866-7, pages 300-2.
†In point of fact the camp-ground was in Cape Elizabeth, on the grounds now occupied by the Rolling Mills.

FIRST MAINE INFANTRY.

COLONEL NATHANIEL J. JACKSON.

Mustered into U. S. service, May 3, 1861, for three months. Sent to Washington, June 1st.

When the call for troops was made, April 15, 1861, there were thirty-five "volunteer companies" or "active and uniformed" militia in the State of Maine. Governor Washburn ordered these to fill their ranks by recruiting, and nineteen of them did so. The other sixteen failed, and so lost their identity. It is noteworthy that five of these thirty-five were Portland companies, and that all five filled their ranks mostly with Portland men, many days before the state and national officers could arm and equip them. The companies were the

Portland Light Infantry,
Portland Mechanic Blues,
Portland Light Guards,
Portland Rifle Corps,
Portland Rifle Guards.

Lewiston claims that the Lewiston Light Infantry (Co. F, 1st Me.) was the first to volunteer. Gen. Beal also claims the honor for his company, the Norway Light Infantry (Co. G, 1st Me.) We give below the Rifle Guards' claim, as stated by Lieut. Wm. M. Quimby.*

I claim to be the first man in the State of Maine to volunteer in the war of the rebellion. On Tuesday evening, January 8, 1861, after the steamer Star of the West was fired upon by the rebels investing Fort Sumter, I arose in the meeting of the Guards, called by Capt. Wm. M. Shaw, at my suggestion, and stated my views in regard to the war which I felt certain was about to be inaugurated. I urged with all my power that the company should make haste and place itself on

*Quimby was commissioned captain in the regular army after his service in the 1st Maine. He was crippled for life at battle of Cedar Mountain, August 9, 1862, and died in 1876.

PORTLAND SOLDIERS AND SAILORS.

record as the first company to volunteer. The meeting was not a very full one, but the members present, with one exception, voted to volunteer. I was much vexed because I could not get a unanimous vote. There the matter rested till the day after the reception of the news of the attack on Fort Sumter. I saw Capt. Shaw, and urged him to call another meeting. He was as ready as myself, and set about it at a good deal of inconvenience, as he had to hunt up every member. At this meeting (Tuesday, April 16) the enthusiasm was tremendous. As soon as it was called to order, I arose and urged the company to volunteer its services. I was most ably seconded by Capt. Shaw, Lieuts. Estes, Merrill and Marston, and many of the non-commissioned officers. The result was that the company volunteered, by a unanimous vote, to offer its services to the State, in anticipation of a call from the general government. [Extract from letter of Capt. Quimby.]

Lieut. Quimby was appointed messenger to go to Augusta, and formally tender the services of the company. He did so and returned immediately with recruiting rolls in his hands. The other Portland companies had to wait for their blank rolls to come, and while they were waiting, "the Guards," in the language of one of the men, "was filling up as fast as the men could write their names on the roll, or one hundred and eighty men in about an hour."

The Rifle Guards enlisted double the number required, and an additional company was necessarily formed, composed largely of residents of Saccarappa, where Lieut. Quimby was wont to spend much of his time courting a young lady.

We remark in passing that this company had gained considerable notoriety, and had probably made itself unpopular with the majority of our citizens, by suppressing the "Neal Dow" or "John Robbins" riot, June 2, 1855. But when the call was made for troops to go to war, there came a reaction in its favor. "Bloody Guards" was no longer spoken in derision.

It will be noticed that Portland furnished six companies of the ten sent in answer to the first call for troops—75,000 three months volunteers.

As before stated, the men were ready long before the State or U. S. could arm and clothe them. After remaining "in quarters" in the halls and large rooms of the city, they were sent May 8, to camp upon a field in East Deering, between the Marine Hospital and Grand Trunk Railway, south of the county road. Here a malignant type of measles broke out, prostrating a hundred men and delaying the departure of the regiment. The remainder of the time was spent on Meridian Hill, Washington, doing guard duty and learning how to grumble and swear.

The Portland officers in this regiment were:
Lieut.-Colonel, Albion Witham,
Major, George G. Bailey,
Quarter-master, William S. Dodge,
Chaplain, George Knox,
Surgeon, Wentworth R. Richardson.

Co. A (PORTLAND LIGHT INFANTRY).
Captain, George W. Tukey.
1st Lieutenant, George H. Chadwell.
2d Lieutenant, Charles L. McAllister.

Co. B (MECHANIC BLUES).
Captain, Charles Walker.
1st Lieutenant, Charles J. Pennell.
2d Lieutenant, James M. Black.

Co. C (LIGHT GUARDS).
Captain, Menzies R. Fessenden.
1st Lieutenant, William P. Jordan.
2d Lieutenant, Benjamin M. Redlon.

PORTLAND SOLDIERS AND SAILORS.   7

Co. D (Rifle Corps).
Captain, Charles H. Meserve.
1st Lieutenant, William A. Pearce.
2d Lieutenant, George H. Bailey.

Co. E (Rifle Guards).
Captain, William M. Shaw.
1st Lieutenant, Albert H. Estes.
2d Lieutenant, John M. Marston.

Co. I (2d Co. of Rifle Guards).
Captain, William M. Quimby.
1st Lieutenant, Nehemiah T. Furbish.

The Second Maine regiment, rendezvoused in Bangor. According to the Adjutant-General's report, there were twenty-three Portland men among its "original members." Horatio Staples, the well-known dry goods dealer, was 1st Lieut. of Co. G, but hailed from Bangor then.

The Third (Gen. Howard's), was a Kennebec regiment, and rendezvoused at Augusta. Not a single Portland name appears on its list of original members, and no Portland officer at any time of its long service. They don't send to Portland for help down on the Kennebec.

The Fourth (Gen. Berry's), was organized at Rockland. There were only three Portlanders among the original members. Dr. Hunkins, who lived here after the war, was surgeon, hailing then from Windham. Solomon J. Stearns, of Portland, "joined as Lieutenant" of Co. F, January 1, 1862.

FIFTH MAINE INFANTRY.

COL. MARK H. DUNNELL, OF PORTLAND.

Mustered in June 23 and 24, 1861, for three years. Sent to Washington, June 26.

There were three Portland companies here:

Co. F, Capt. George P. Sherwood.
Co. G, Capt. Henry G. Thomas.
Co. H, Capt. Edward A. Scammon.

Sherwood was wounded and invalided at Bull Run. Thomas eventually became Brigadier-General and is now in the regular army. Scammon was promoted to Colonel, lost his health and died.

Three Portland men were successively appointed Adjutants:

Charles Whitman,
George W. Graffam,
George W. Bicknell.

Whitman resigned shortly after appointment and re-entered the navy in which he had previously served. Graffam entered the regular army, died 1882. Bicknell was for many years pastor of the India St. Universalist Church.

The other Portland officers were Maj. Henry R. Millett, hailing from Palmyra, and now living at Gorham, but well known from a long residence here after the war.

Capt. Thomas J. Sawyer.
" Alburn P. Harris.
" George E. Brown.
" Nathan Walker.
" Daniel C. Clark.

1st Lieut. William E. Stevens.
" Charles O. Waterhouse.
" George W. Martin.

1st Lieut. Ambrose S. Dyer.
" Richard C. Shannon.
2d Lieut. J. Augustine Grenier.
" Frank G. Patterson.
" Robert J. McPherson.
" Samuel Munson.

Of this long list, only Capt. Brown, the photographer, remains here now. Clark was mortally wounded at Spottsylvania. He was one of the most lovable of men.

Shannon and Munson were promoted, by the President, to the general staff.

Col. Dunnell is credited to Portland, though he resigned after holding his Colonel's commission a few months; then went west and next appeared as congressman from Minnesota, where his remarkable dealing with the "salary grab" bill gave him great notoriety. In the language of a newspaper of the period, he worked like a beaver for the passage of the bill; piously voted against it when he found his vote was not needed, pocketed the spoils and telegraphed home to "*begin hauling sand*" for the new house.

The Fifth had a long and creditable service after they once got started in the right way. Especially noteworthy were the assault on Marye's Heights (Fredericksburg) May 3, 1863; the charge at Rappahannock station, Nov. 7, 1863, when as many rebels were taken prisoners as the Union party making the assault; and the grand charge under Gen. Upton, at Spottsylvania, May 10, 1864.

The term of service of the original members expired while the regiment was with Grant in front of Petersburg; the recruits were consolidated with the 6th and 7th Maine shortly after and called the 1st Maine Veterans.

Few Maine regiments were engaged in so many battles or took such prominent part in them as did the old Fifth.

The Fifth was in the famous Sixth corps. The list of the battles begins away back with the first Bull Run, takes in the Peninsula campaign, Crampton Gap and Antietam, Md., Fredericksburg, Gettysburg, Rappahannock Station, Spottsylvania, and Cold Harbor.

Gen. Upton, in his parting address to them, said: "You "have captured the battle-flags of five of the proudest "regiments in the Confederate service; and while inflict- "ing a loss equal to your own, you have in addition cap- "tured more prisoners than you have names on your rolls."

The Sixth regiment was recruited in the eastern part of the state but rendezvoused at Portland. Mustered in July 15, 1861, for three years and sent to Washington two or three days later. There were twenty-seven Portland men among the original members, and Chaplain Zenas Thompson and 1st Lieut. Frank H. Burnham are also credited to Portland.

The Seventh regiment had one "Portland company," Capt. Charles H. Gilman's, Co. G, but many of the men came from suburban towns. There were, however, fifty-seven Portlanders among the original members, and Col. Mason is credited to Portland, though more properly his hail should have been U. S. Army. For other Portland officers we have Captain Joseph H. Walker who died in the service, Captains William M. Cushman and George McGinley. The last served three months in the 1st Maine and was transferred to the 1st Veterans, and so served through the entire war. Capt. Albert A. Nickerson who also served long and well made Portland his home for a number of years. Lieut. Geo. B. Knight and Luther B. Crosby also hailed from Portland.

The Eighth regiment had but six Portland names in the original membership, and one of these was Lieut. Charles E. Howard, formerly Sergeant of Co. C, 1st Maine, an experienced drill-master. He died in the service.

The Ninth regiment had fifteen Portland men in the original membership, including five officers, viz.: Col. Rishworth Rich, Adjutant James C. M. Furbish, Lieuts. John L. Emerson, Henry A. Gray and Joshua G. Ross. Charles F. Weeks, of New Sharon, who joined as recruit in 1862, and worked his way speedily to a captaincy, changed his residence to Portland as he rose. Nothing weak about that.

TENTH MAINE INFANTRY.

Col. George L. Beal.

Mustered in October 3 and 4, 1861, for two and three years. Left for Baltimore, Md., October 6th.

This regiment was the reorganization of the First. It has four Portland companies, viz.:

B (Mechanic Blues), Capts. Black and Turner.
C (Light Guards), Capt. Jordan.
E (Rifle Guards), Capts. Estes, Latham, Cloudman and Sargent.
I (Rifle Guards), Capts. Furbish and (Mayhew of Saccarappa).

PORTLAND SOLDIERS AND SAILORS.

The old Light Infantry and Rifle Corps were practically disbanded on returning from the field with the 1st Maine, and their company organizations were not present in the 10th.

The Portland officers were:
    Major, Charles Walker,
    Quartermaster, William S. Dodge,
    Surgeon, Daniel O. Perry,
    Assistant Surgeon, Josiah F. Day, jr.,
    Chaplain, George Knox,
    Captain, James M. Black,
    " Alfred L. Turner,
    " William P. Jordan,
    " Albert H. Estes,
    " Cyrus Latham,
    " Andrew C. Cloudman,
    " Herbert R. Sargent,
    " Nehemiah T. Furbish,
    1st Lieut., Charles W. Roberts,
    " Benjamin F. Whitney,
    " Benjamin M. Redlon,
    " Charles F. King,
    " John M. Gould,
    2d Lieut., Reuben Alexander,
    " Marcus Delano,
    " Joseph H. Perley, jr.,
    " Henry F. Smith,
    " John T. Simpson.

Cloudman and Furbish were killed. Alexander died of wounds. Perley died of consumption. Sargent and

Turner were wounded. Walker, Dodge, Estes, Latham and Simpson resigned on account of sickness. Roberts was promoted to Adjutant of the 17th Maine.

The Tenth was more distinctively a Portland regiment than any other from this state. A half of the officers and nearly a half of the enlisted men came from Portland and suburban towns; and Col. Beal, who was its Colonel from first to last, though born in the town of Norway, had lived in Portland a number of years before the war.

The regiment was one for Portland to be proud of. It achieved the honor of being one of eleven in all the Army of the Potomac that had "earned high commendation."

The fight it made at Cedar Mountain, Aug. 9, 1862, was most sanguinary, and that at Antietam was stubborn and bloody again. At the time of its discharge it had lost by bullet more than any other Maine regiment. Seventy-three men were killed or died of wounds against forty-eight from disease, reversing completely the common rule that disease kills more than the bullet.

The Tenth had the misfortune of serving under Gen. John Pope, and being most wretchedly led, or misled by its general officers in every battle.

On the expiration of its term of service, May 2, 1863, there were about two hundred and fifty three years recruits who were organized into the "Tenth Maine Battalion." They served as a Headquarters guard of the Twelfth Army corps, Gen. Slocum's, until May, 1864, when they were consolidated with the Twenty-ninth regiment. This battalion was a model command and followed the Twelfth corps to Chancellorsville and Gettysburg, and to Tennessee.

The first ten regiments, were "raised, subsisted and completely fitted out at the expense of the state." The five infantry regiments that followed, and also the First cavalry and six batteries, were raised at the direct expense of the U. S. government.

The companies of these latter regiments were not recruited so largely from special cities and towns; there consequently were no distinctively Portland companies in the Eleventh to Fifteenth regiments, or in the cavalry and artillery.

The Eleventh regiment had twenty-five Portland men among the original members. William M. Shaw, who had been Captain of the Portland Rifle Guards in the First Maine, was Major and Lieutenant-Colonel. Charles J. Pennell, formerly of the Blues in the First Maine, was the Adjutant. There were also promoted from the ranks of the old First Maine:

Captain, Woodbury S. Pennell,
1st Lieut., John M. Beal,
" Charles H. Scott.

TWELFTH MAINE INFANTRY.

COLONEL GEORGE F. SHEPLEY, OF PORTLAND.

Mustered in November 15 to 20, 1861, for three years. Left Portland for Lowell, Mass., Nov. 24, 1861, and went aboard transport for Fortress Monroe, Va., Jan. 2, 1862, thence to Ship Island, La., February 4.

There were seventy-three Portland names on the list of original members. Captain George H. Chadwell's company, B, was reckoned as the Portland company.

The Portland officers were:

Colonel, George F. Shepley,
Adjutant, William Wallace Deane,
Quarter-master, Horatio N. Jose,
" " Charles D. Webb,
Chaplain, William Brown,
Captain, George H. Chadwell,
" Menzies R. Fessenden,
" John W. Dana,
" Moses M. Robinson,
1st Lieut., Elbridge G. Bolton,
" Charles F. Little,
" Simeon Bolivar Wiggin,
" Horatio Hight (Scarboro),*
2d Lieut., George E. Andrews (Scarboro),*
" Gustavus Smith.

Fessenden, Chadwell, Wiggin and Andrews had served in the 1st Maine.

The late Henry T. Carter, Esq., one of our well-known citizens, was a member of this regiment.

Soon after landing in Louisiana, Col. Shepley was made Military Governor of the state and Brigadier General. The regiment engaged in a number of minor expeditions, and in 1863 took part in the Teche campaign and in the siege and assault of Port Hudson. They were not actively engaged in the Red River expedition of 1864, but came North in July and joined Sheridan's army, and so participated in the battles of "the Valley"; in all of which they did good service and met heavy losses.

*Now residing in Portland.

After all this the regiment received six new companies, and a very different set of men came home as the 12th Maine from those who went out by that name; a remark that applies to other regiments we can mention.

THIRTEENTH MAINE INFANTRY.

COLONEL NEAL DOW, OF PORTLAND.

Mustered in Dec. 13, 1861, for three years. Sent from Augusta to Ship Island, La., via Fortress Monroe, in Feb., 1862.

The Thirteenth had sixty-seven Portlanders among the original members.

The Portland officers were :
    Colonel, Neal Dow,
    Asst. Surgeon, Seth C. Gordon (Gorham),
    Chaplain, Henry D. Moore,
    Captain, Charles R. March,
        "   Reuben T. Jordan,
        "   Joshua L. Sawyer,
        "   Augustine W. Clough,
        "   Isaiah Randall,
    1st Lieut., John T. Sherburne,
        "   William P. Freeman,
        "   Aaron Ring,
        "   William E. Simmons,
    2d Lieut., William H. Sargent.

Colonel Dow was made Brigadier-General in April, 1862. Dr. Gordon was promoted to a Louisiana regiment, and Chaplain Moore, after spending a night and day on the deep, seasick and sorry, returned home, laden with the benedictions of Gen. Butler. But we beg to be excused from quoting the exact words of Old Ben.

This regiment had the ill luck of being assigned to guard duty and garrisoning forts about all its term of service, and for the most part it was unpleasant and unhealthy business. Excepting some guerrilla warfare, etc., they had no fighting of consequence till April, 1864, when they were left alone on the flank of the army, while a strange regiment fled, its Colonel taking cover under a corn crib or some such thing. All this up Red River with Gen. Banks looking on,—funny fighting thought he and the 13th.

The regiment came North in July, 1864, and defended Sheridan's wagons in "the Valley." There was no three-years regiment from Maine that had so little fighting and few that had such a dreary time of it on the whole.

The Fourteenth regiment had one Portlander on its original roll, Capt. George H. Cheney. Lieut. George Webster came in later, and both resigned.

The Fifteenth regiment had fifteen Portlanders in it at first. Captain Charles S. Ilsley was the only officer we furnished. He served his term, entered the regular army, and is now Captain in 7th U. S. cavalry.

Gen. Benj. B. Murray, of the 15th, resided in Portland while he was U. S. Marshal, and Captain Henry A. Shorey is now in the custom-house.

The Sixteenth regiment had about* a dozen Portland men in it; one of whom was that odd stick, William H. Broughton, the great checker player, who rose from the ranks to be Captain of Co. D, and served with honor and distinction to the end of the war.

*The Adjutant-General did not tabulate the original members by towns and cities after the 15th regiment.

Lieut. Fred H. Beecher, of the 16th, a young man of great promise, who was commissioned in the regular army after the war, and was killed by Indians, could without much violence be reckoned a Portlander, as could also Lieut. William T. Dodge, also of the 16th, and of the regular army.

SEVENTEENTH MAINE INFANTRY.
COLONEL THOMAS A. ROBERTS, OF PORTLAND.

Mustered in August 18, 1862, for three years. Sent to Washington, August 20, and assigned to the Third Army corps.

There were two that were called Portland companies, though the majority of their men came from other towns.

The regiment is as well known as any in our city. Portland gave a long list of able officers and men to this famous organization, and they did their part in making the 17th the glorious old regiment it was.

Colonel, Thomas A. Roberts,
" Charles P. Mattocks,
Lieut.-Colonel, Charles B. Merrill,
Adjutant, Charles W. Roberts,
" Putnam S. Boothby,
Quartermaster, Jacob Thatcher Waterhouse,
" Josiah Remick,
Surgeon, Nahum A. Hersom (Sanford),
Chaplain, Harvey Hersey,
" Joseph F. Lovering,
Captain, William H. Savage,
" George W. Martin,
" Benjamin C. Pennell,
" Granville F. Sparrow,
" Edward Moore,

PORTLAND SOLDIERS AND SAILORS. 19

Captain, John C. Perry,
" Ellis M. Sawyer (Cape Elizabeth),
" William H. Green,
" George W. Verrill,
" Albion Hersey (Paris),
" Joseph A. Perry,
" Edwin B. Houghton,
" Andrew J. Stinson (Kittery),
" James O. Thompson,
1st Lieut., James M. Brown,
" James S. Roberts,
" Edward H. Crie,
" Newton Whitten,
" Fred. A. Sawyer,
" Henry L. Bartels,
2d Lieut., Stephen Graffam,
" James M. Safford,
" Horace B. Cummings,
" Thomas Snowman.

Pennell, Sawyer, Brown and Roberts were killed. Waterhouse died in the service. Gen. Mattocks had a checkered and eventful career, including capture, escape, and recapture, which will pay perusal. (See page 413, Volume I., 1864-5, Adjutant-General's Report.) The names of twenty-seven engagements are inscribed on the colors, the most important of which are Chancellorsville, Gettysburg, Locust Grove, the Wilderness, etc., and the battles before Petersburg. The losses were very heavy and the fighting always good. Portland has always been proud of the 17th, and with good reason. No other regiment took so much "brain" from our city.

Fred. Bosworth, for whom our No. 2 Post of the Grand Army of the Republic was named, served in this regiment, and was killed at Wapping Heights, Aug. 23, 1863.

(For 18th Maine, see First Heavy Artillery.)

The Nineteenth regiment was raised on the Kennebec, and like the 3d Maine, it made a most honorable record, without any help from Portland till late in the war. Isaac W. Starbird, its last Colonel, lived with us a number of years after discharge. William L. Gerrish, transferred from the 5th Independent Co., earned a Second Lieutenancy in January, 1865, but died a few weeks later.

The Twentieth regiment (Ames's and afterward Gen. Chamberlain's) was organized at Portland in August, 1862, but the officers and men came from other places, with hardly an exception. These exceptions were notable. Gen. John M. Brown, President of our Monument Association, began his military career here as Adjutant; and Wm. E. Donnell stepped into Brown's shoes on his promotion. Dr. Abner O. Shaw was the surgeon. Holman S. Melcher, formerly of Topsham, who has for many years been a wholesale grocer here, rose from the ranks to be Captain and Brevet-Major, and to enjoy the reputation of being one of the bravest men in the corps.

The Twenty-first, Twenty-second, Twenty-third and Twenty-fourth, were nine months regiments raised in the autumn of 1862. The word Portland is not seen on their rolls, though Judge Virgin who was Colonel of the 23d, and Lieut. Henry B. Cleaves, also of the 23d, reside here now.

TWENTY-FIFTH MAINE INFANTRY.

COL. FRANCIS FESSENDEN, OF PORTLAND.

Mustered in Sept. 29th, 1862, for nine months. Sent to Washington, Oct. 16th.

Three Portland companies entered this regiment, A, B and H. Co. A was more distinctively a Portland company than any which had been raised since the 1st Maine regiment. It had in its ranks a great many young men who have since become our "well-known" or "prominent" citizens. One cannot read the roll without a smile; and herein lies the foundation of that harmless bit of irony so often spoken, "The Bloody Twenty-fifth ";—for it was one of the best equipped regiments that ever left the state in the item of "*brain*," yet it was its misfortune to be kept guarding Long Bridge, "digging dirt," and picketing on the outskirts of Washington during its entire service. Consequently when the regiment came back without having been ordered into battle, many who had carefully staid at home criticised the regiment harshly. Any one who ever saw the regiment knows that it needs no defender.

The Portland officers were:

Colonel, Francis Fessenden,
Lieut.-Colonel, Charles E. Shaw,
Major, Alexander M. Tolman,
Chaplain, Edward B. Furbish,
Captain A, Frank L. Jones,
" " George H. Abbott,
" B, Edward Nelson Greely,
" C, Whitman Sawyer (Raymond),
" H, Charles C. Chase,

1st Lieut. A, Charles B. Hall,
" B, Levi M. Prince,
" H, John H. Knight,
" K, Isaac D. Sawyer (Standish),
2d Lieut. A, Cyrus H. Illsley,
" E, Frank G. Stevens,
" I, George O. Gosse.

The Twenty-sixth regiment had no Portlanders in it.

TWENTY-SEVENTH MAINE INFANTRY.
COLONEL RUFUS P. TAPLEY.

Mustered in September 30, 1862, for nine months. Sent to Washington October 20th.

This regiment rendezvoused at Portland, but had only one individual credited to us on the rolls. This was Adjutant Edward M. Rand, now a well-known member of the Cumberland Bar. The history of this regiment is quite like that of the 25th, with which it was brigaded; but the men escaped the abuse which fell to the lot of the 25th, first by having no great expectations formed concerning them, and last by volunteering to stay over the time of their enlistment. Tradition runs that our townsman Rand was an earnest advocate of the last project. They luckily came home just when the country was wild with joy over the victory at Gettysburg.

The Twenty-eighth regiment (the last of the nine months organizations) had no Portland names on the rolls.

TWENTY-NINTH MAINE INFANTRY.

COL. GEORGE L. BEAL.
(Re-organization of Tenth Maine.)

Mustered in Nov. 13, to Dec. 17, 1863, for three years. Left Augusta for New Orleans Jan. 31, 1864, and assigned to the Nineteenth Army corps.

This regiment did not rendezvous at Portland; but carrying as it did the traditions of the First and Tenth of which it was the successor we have always claimed a special interest in it. It was the first regiment raised in Maine under the "Veteran" order. The officers and non-commissioned officers with few exceptions had been in service before. The men came from almost every town in the state and the local coloring is consequently faint. Companies C and E are, however, reckoned as Portland companies.

The Tenth battalion was consolidated with this regiment as before noted.

The Portland officers were:
    Major, John M. Gould,
    Adjutant, Alpheus L. Greene,
    Quarter-master,* William E. St. John,
    Surgeon, Josiah F. Day, jr.,
    Chaplain, George Knox,
    Captain, B, Benjamin M. Redlon,
        "   C, William P. Jordan,
        "   E, John M. Beal,
        "   F, Alfred L. Turner,
    1st Lieut. D, Charles Fred King,
        "   E, Charles C. Graham,
    2d Lieut. C, Henry M. Smith,
        "   E, Cyrus T. Waterhouse,
        "   F,* Cornelius D. Maynard.

*Not mustered in as officers because of reduced size of the regiment.

The regiment was sent on the Red River expedition, March, 1864, and did so well in the first battle that Col. Beal was jumped over the other Colonels and put in command of the brigade. In July the larger part of the Nineteenth corps were sent to Virginia, and the regiment took prominent part in the battles in the Valley, under Sheridan. The long fight at Cedar Creek, when Sheridan was "twenty miles away," is considered by the men of the regiment as the most stubborn and best fought every way of all their engagements. The regiment was sent to South Carolina after the war and was not mustered out until June, 1866.

Since the war, the members of the First, Tenth and Twenty-ninth regiments, including the Tenth battalion, have formed an Association, and call themselves one regiment, the "First-Tenth-Twenty-ninth"; the history of the four organizations being continuous. They are now building upon Long Island, Casco Bay, a hall for reunion purposes, the benefits of which will be watched by other regiments with great interest.

THIRTIETH MAINE INFANTRY.
COLONEL FRANCIS FESSENDEN.

Mustered in Dec. 15th, 1863, to January 9, 1864, for three years. Left Augusta for New Orleans February 7, 1864, and assigned to the Nineteenth Army corps.

Like the Twenty-ninth this was a "Veteran" regiment; it carried the traditions of the old Twenty-fifth, and recruited all over the state. The officers and non-commissioned officers were almost all of them "Veterans." No company had a majority of men from any one town, but Portland men predominated in Co. I, Capt. Frank L.

Jones, whom we have already seen in the Twenty-fifth. The other Portland officers beside Col. Fessenden and Capt. Jones were:

Adjutant, Charles F. Larrabee,
Quarter-master, Frank H. Coffin,
Asst. Surgeon, Thomas H. Breslin,
Captain, Whitman Sawyer,
" Levi M. Prince,
1st Lieut., Henry B. Cleaves,
" Charles B. Hall,
2d Lieut., Franklin E. Holmes,
" Lewis F. Cummings,
" Burrett H. Beale,
" William H. Motley.

Larrabee and Hall were commissioned in the regular army after the war. Lieut.-Col. Royal E. Whitman, whose business was in Portland before the war, was also commissioned in the regular army.

The regiment took part in the battles of the Red River campaign, in one of which, "Cane River Crossing," Col. Fessenden won his Brigadier-General's star, but lost his leg. He was commanding the brigade at the time, and it is worth noting as a curious coincidence that this brigade, late in the war, fell to the command of his brother, Brig.-Gen. James D. Fessenden. Coming north in July with the Nineteenth corps, the Thirtieth went first to Deep Bottom, then to the Valley where Sheridan set them to guarding his long trains.

The remnants of the Thirteenth Maine were consolidated with the Thirtieth, in Nov., 1864, at which time the companies were reorganized.

The Thirty-first was a new regiment, though many of the officers and non-commissioned officers were "Veterans." It was organized at Augusta, and recruited in the eastern part of the state. There were no Portlanders among the original members. The Thirty-second Maine was consolidated with it in December, 1864. (See Thirty-second Maine.)

The Thirty-second Maine was the last full regiment raised in our state. The officers and non-commissioned officers were for the most part Veterans. Six companies were hurried off to the front and assigned to the Ninth Army corps, April 20, 1864, the other four went later. Captain Chadwell's and Captain Sargent's companies had a large number of Portland men in them. The Portland officers were:

Lieut.-Col. John Marshall Brown,
Captain C, Herbert R. Sargent,
" H, George H. Chadwell,
" H, Thomas P. Beals,
2d Lieut. H, Henry G. Mitchell.

Col. Brown had served in the Twentieth and on General staff. Captain Chadwell in the First and Twelfth, Captain Sargent in the First and Tenth, and Captain Beals in the Seventh. Brown and Sargent were wounded, Chadwell died, and Mitchell was captured. The regiment had an exceedingly "rough" service under Grant in the Wilderness, and so on to the battle of the Crater or Mine explosion from which they emerged with only fifty men. The remnant of the regiment was transferred to the Thirty-first Maine in December after a "short and active career" during which it "did comparatively as much and as hard fighting as any other organization."

Thirty "unassigned" or independent companies were raised to serve one, two and three years from Sept., 1864, to April, 1865, of which the Twenty-sixth and Twenty-ninth were from this city.

The Twenty-sixth unassigned company of Infantry, Capt. George L. Fickett, was recruited in Portland and half of the men were residents of our city. The company was finally assigned to the "1st Battalion." Mustered in April 5th, 1865, for one year. They served out their time in the Shenandoah Valley, Washington and South Carolina; but the war was virtually over before they arrived on the field.

The Twenty-ninth company was raised in Portland. Capt. Aaron Ring, Lieuts. Fred D. Lovell and T. Gilman Webster. About half the men were Portlanders. They were mustered in April 25th, 1865, and mustered out three weeks later without having left the state.

The First Maine Veterans was a regiment made by consolidation of the veterans and recruits of the Fifth, Sixth, and Seventh regiments. We have already noticed the Portland officers excepting:

Dr. Stillman P. Getchell at that time hailing from Vienna, and 2d Lieut. Edward J. Dolan, a young Irish American who had been a Sergeant in the Fifth Maine.

There are not many Portland names on the rolls of the "First Vets," and we grieve to remark that against those few are every species of "black mark" that Adj.-Gen. Hodsdon could invent.

A company of sharpshooters was raised in Maine, November, 1861, by our townsman, the late James D. Fessenden, who starting here gave a long and valuable service to the country, mostly in western armies, and finally came back wearing the Brig.-General's star, to command his brother Frank's brigade in Sheridan's army.

Daniel L. Cummings was 2d Lieut., and afterward 1st Lieut. of this company, which was known as Co. D, Second U. S. Sharpshooters.

There were also Coast Guards, Militia companies and what all, for which see the A. G. reports.

FIRST MAINE CAVALRY.

Colonel John Goddard; succeeded by Allen, Doughty (killed), and Charles H. Smith.

This fine regiment, which did as much for the good name of our state as any we sent out, had one Portland company, composed, in fact, of men from almost everywhere. As the war went on, many recruits were sent out, of which Portland contributed her part.

Late in 1863 and early in 1864, eight companies of cavalry were enlisted in Maine and called the First District of Columbia Cavalry. After many vicissitudes, especially after being nearly all captured in a raid, which reflected greater credit upon the rebel General, Wade Hampton, than it did upon the officer in command of the D. C. Cavalry, they were transferred to the First Maine Cavalry.

First and last, therefore, there were men enough in the regiment to make a respectable brigade.

PORTLAND SOLDIERS AND SAILORS.

The officers from Portland, in both regiments, including those who have taken up their residence here since the war, were:

Lieut.-Col., Stephen Boothby,
Major, Sidney W. Thaxter (Bangor),
Adjutant, Jarvis C. Stevens,
Quarter-master, Edward M. Patten,
Commissary, Eustis C. Bigelow,
Asst. Surgeon, George J. Northrop,
Captain C, Andrew M. Benson (Oldtown, 1st D. C.),
" F, Nathan Mayhew,
" F, Walstein Phillips,
" G, Charles C. Chase (1st D. C.),
" I, Thomas C. Webber (1st D. C.),
1st Lieut. D, Edward P. Merrill,
" E, John H. Goddard,
" F, William Harris,
" H, James McGuire,
" K, Charles W. Ford (Bristol),
2d Lieut. F, Lorenzo White.

Boothby, Phillips, and Harris were killed. The regiment was engaged in thirty-six battles, and in many of them there was fighting of the kind that belongs to infantrymen. Their first engagement was at Middletown, in the Valley, during Banks' retreat May 1862. It was against infantry and artillery, a thing unheard of in those days. At Brandy Station, June 9, 1863, they had another day to be remembered. Eight days later at Aldie, Col. Doughty fell. After these hard battles the foot-soldiers had a confidence in the cavalrymen not enjoyed before.

In 1864, under Sheridan at Ground Squirrel church, another terrible day was passed during which our own brave Boothby was mortally wounded as was also the rebel General J. E. B. Stuart. In truth from 1862 to 1865 there was plenty of marching, skirmishing and hard fighting for this well trained command. They earned the name of being "among the best in the service."

The Second Cavalry had few Portland names. Dr. Rodolph L. Dodge was the only officer from Portland; serving there as 2d Lieut.

The First Maine Heavy Artillery, known at first as the Eighteenth Infantry, and called the "First Heavy" for short, had hardly a Portland name except that of Lieut.-Colonel Thomas H. Talbot, well known in our city before the war but not residing here since. Lieut.-Col. Zimro A. Smith who was for a number of years editor of the Portland Press served the entire term of the regiment.

Of the seven batteries of mounted artillery all but the First belonged in the Army of the Potomac. The First was raised in Portland. Here Albert W. Bradbury, at that time hailing from Eastport, entered upon his military career which ended in his being made Brevet-Colonel and Chief of Artillery of the Nineteenth Army corps of which corps the First battery was a part. Portland also furnished thirty-one of the original members of the battery and about as many more recruits at various times.

The Second battery had six original members that hailed from Portland including Lieuts. Samuel Paine and Samuel Fessenden; the last was the younger brother of Gens. Jas.

D. and Frank, and one of the most genial and open-hearted young men that ever wore blue. He fell at the second Bull Run.

Not a single Portland man's name appears on the roll of the Third battery until March 10th, 1864, when George E. Skillings comes in with a 2d Lieut.'s commission and he is soon after promoted to 1st Lieut. These Portland boys seem to have had a taste for commissions.

The Fourth battery, likewise, gives no hint of the existence of Portland, except through "Gus" Fox, one of the old "Hard Dees" of the First Maine, who starting as Corporal, rose in time to be Second Lieutenant, and "hung to it" from first to last. There were also Lieutenants Lucius M. S. Haynes and Henry C. Haynes, brothers, who lived in Portland many years when boys, and received proper castigation at the hands of "Craney" Jones, their schoolmaster, in spite of their being minister's sons.

The Fifth battery had eighteen original members from Portland, including Lieuts. William F. Twitchell and Ezra Clark jr. Dr. Charles O. Hunt, now surgeon in charge of Maine General Hospital, was Second Lieutenant of this battery. Captain Leppien is also credited to Portland, though he was not a citizen of Maine at all. Leppien was one of the finest soldiers ever commissioned from Maine, and he disciplined the Fifth battery till there was nothing better either in the regulars or Rhode Island. He fell at Chancellorsville, and Twitchell at the Second Bull Run.

The Sixth battery had thirteen Portland names on the Nov. '62 muster roll. Here again we see the *penchant* of our folks for commissions.

  Captain, Edwin B. Dow,
  1st Lieut., Samuel Thurston,
  2d Lieut., Orville W. Merrill,
    " William H. Gallison,
    " John G. Deane.

Sterling Dow also came within one of a commission, getting as high as Q. M. Sergeant.

The Seventh battery organized in 1864 had ten or a dozen Portland men in it.

First Lieut., Loren E. Bundy, was the only officer that we can claim. They were in the Ninth corps.

RE-CAPTURE OF THE "CALEB CUSHING."

On the afternoon of June 25, 1863, a "gang of pirates," as we called them in those days, originally from the rebel steamer "Florida," peacefully entered Portland harbor in the fishing schooner "Archer," which they had captured a few days before. Early in the morning of the 26th, they easily surprised and captured the Revenue Cutter "Caleb Cushing," and put to sea with her, the "Archer" following. The details of their being becalmed and re-captured by a small fleet of steamers and tug boats, hastily manned, are narrated on pages 15 to 23 of Adj.-Gen.'s Report, 1863. We only wish here to emphasize the fact that "Capt. Jake" McLellan was mayor of our city then, and the late Jedediah Jewett collector of the port; and life was worth living that morning if only to see the tremendous energy of those two men.

Furthermore it should be known that the "pirates" couldn't find the ammunition, or at least the shot and shell. What would have become of the "Forest City" and the "Tiger" had they found it, is not very doubtful. The "Chesapeake" was better fitted for a naval engagement; but we wish to remark, what is not stated elsewhere, that Capt. Charles F. Knapp, at present the Shipping Commissioner of our port, was aboard and really in command by force of superior will, though Leighton, the naval constructor, was given the command, and Col. Mason of the Seventh Maine was "commanding" the infantry. When the pirates fired their guns loaded with spikes, old iron and cheese-rinds at the "Chesapeake," Capt. Willets of the steamer inquired what to do, Knapp insisted that we should "run her down" and board her. Firing six-pounder field guns at a craft like the "Cushing" was too much like nonsense to him. The enemy seeing this, set fire to the cutter and took to their boats. Fortunately for them the "Forest City" with officers of the Seventeenth U.S.Infantry aboard, picked them up. How much "picking up" Knapp would have done is one of the unsolved problems of this case.

Four war vessels were built here during the war.

The gunboat Kineo, six guns, 507 tons, launched Oct. 9, 1861. The contract time was one hundred days. Built by the late Joseph W. Dyer, at Ferry Village. Engines furnished in New York.

The "double ender" side-wheel steamer Agawam, twelve guns, 974 tons, launched April 21st, 1863. Built by George W. Lawrence, at his yard near where the Forest City Sugar Refinery now stands. Engines built by the Portland Company.

The double ender Pontoosuc, ten guns, 974 tons. Built by G. W. Lawrence, after the Agawam. Engines furnished by the Portland Company.

The light draught, iron-clad monitor Wassuc, two guns, 614 tons, launched in 1864. Built by Geo. W. Lawrence. Motive and turret engines and a large part of the turret works were built by Charles Staples & Son.

Chas. Staples & Son also forged a large amount of iron work for the forts in our harbor. The embrasures of the casemates were particularly heavy and there were many of them.

The Portland Company built a number of fine locomotives for the government and experimented in casting heavy guns. They also furnished the works of the steamer Ella Morse, built at Bath, which was bought by the government and used as a tow boat at New Orleans.

PORTLAND OFFICERS

Not Previously Mentioned.

HORACE ANDERSON, on duty with the U. S. Coast Survey, in South Atlantic States.

NATHAN BARKER, Capt. and Assistant Quartermaster. Dead.

IRA BERRY JR., Captain Fourteenth N. H. He was member of a Mobile, Ala., company on the outbreak of the rebellion, but knew his duty, and did it.

CHARLES H. BOYD of the U. S. Coast Survey, Brevet-Major U. S. A., on staff of Admiral Dupont 1861. Engineer duty in defences of Washington 1862. Engineer of Cavalry corps, Army of Cumberland 1863. A. D. C. to Gen. Geo. H. Thomas 1864–5.

EDWARD DEERING BOYD, Second Colorado Cavalry, 1862; Inspector Cavalry, Gen. Blunt's staff, Missouri; wounded.

PARKER DWIGHT BOYD, Capt. and Commissary of Subsistence, Staff of Gen. Burnside; died 1872.

EUGENE CARTER, Lieut. of Eighth U. S. Infantry; Capt. Twenty-ninth U. S. I. Brevet-Major. Dead.

JOHN C. COBB, now practicing law in Portland, was Colonel of Second Regiment U. S. Colored Engineers (afterward designated as the Ninety-Sixth U. S. C. T.) and commanding a brigade of the Thirteenth Army corps the greater part of his service.

Rev. EPHRAIM C. CUMMINGS, Chaplain Fifteenth Vt.

GEORGE W. EDDY, of the Post-office, was Captain and ...mmissary of Subsistence.

JOHN EDWARDS JR., 2d Lieut. and Capt. Third U. S. Artillery, Brevet-Lieut.-Colonel U. S. A., was conspicuous for his coolness and bravery on many battlefields, beginning with Bull Run. Dead.

FREDERICK W. EMERY, of Emery, Waterhouse & Co., before the war, was promoted Captain and Asst. Adj.-General from the Seventh Kansas regiment.

ZENAS R. FARRINGTON was agent of the Christian Commission.

WILLIAM D. FERNALD, Lieut. in the Veteran Reserve Corps and on duty in the Freedmen's Bureau.

GEORGE FORSAITH, Private D, Tenth Maine and G, Thirteenth Maine, 1st Lieut. Ninety-eighth and Seventy-eighth U. S. C. T.

PATRICK R. GUINEY was a small Irish boy that graced the vicinity of Gorham's Corner in days gone by, if stories we hear are true. He developed manly qualities, went to Boston, became in time Captain and Colonel of the Ninth Mass. and Brevet-Brig.-General.

WILLIAM H. KALOR, 2d Lieut. One Hundred and Third U. S. Colored Troops.

JUDGE ENOCH KNIGHT (formerly of Bridgton), was Captain in Twelfth Maine.

THOMAS J. LITTLE, Lieut. Thirteenth Mass., Captain First Mass. Heavy Artillery.

WILLIAM C. MANNING, private, drummer, corporal, and Seargt.-Maj. First Mass.; 1st Lieut. and Capt. Thirty-fifth U. S. C. T.; Maj. One Hundred and Third U. S. C. T. Now Adjutant of the Twenty-third U. S. I.

JOHN L. MESERVE JR. was 1st Lieut. Eightieth U. S. Colored troops and promoted Captain of Commissary Department. Dead.

JAMES F. MILLER, A. A. G. on Gen. Shepley's staff; military commander, or "Mayor," of New Orleans. Dead

FRANK NOYES, Treasurer Portland Savings Bank, served in a N. Y. regiment and in the Quartermaster's Department. Dead.

GEORGE FREEMAN NOYES, Captain on Gen. Doubleday's staff; Brevet-Lieut.-Col.; author of "*Bivouac and Battle Field.*" Dead.

CHARLES W. OLESON, Private Fifth Maine Battery, Asst. Surgeon Fourteenth U. S. Colored Troops.

REV. EDWARD N. POMEROY, now of Taunton, Mass., was 2d Lieut. of Eighty-first U. S. Colored Troops.

ALBERT H. PURINGTON, Private A, First Me., and B, Twelfth Me.; Captain Ninety-seventh U. S. C. T.

WILLIAM F. RUNDLETT, now residing in Portland, was 2d Lieut. H, Twenty-first Maine.

HENRY STONE, local editor of the Advertiser, was Captain and Asst. Adj.-General.

PETER G. S. TEN BROECK, Surgeon U. S. A. Dead.

LAWRENCE P. VARNUM, Private A, Twenty-Fifth Me., 2d Lieut. Seventy-ninth U. S. C. T.

MARCUS WIGHT JR., graduate of Bowdoin College, and private in Twenty-Ninth Maine regiment, made Portland his residence for many years after the war. He was Lieut. in the Fourth U. S. Colored Cavalry.

PORTLAND SOLDIERS AND SAILORS.

NAVY.

In the long list of names of men furnished to the Navy from Maine, are hundreds credited to Portland. Promotion in the navy, of enlisted men to commissioned officers, was not so common as in the army. The Naval officers were selected in a more conservative way.

Rear Admiral JAMES ALDEN, whose body lies in Eastern Cemetery, was born and resided in Portland.

Rear Admiral GEORGE H. PREBLE, also, was born and resided in Portland.

The deeds of two such conspicuous men cannot be recited in these few pages.

WILLIAM HENRY ANDERSON, Paymaster, was stationed the most of the time in the Sounds of North Carolina, and saw a good deal of fighting.

FRED A. G. BACON, Acting Ensign. Dead.

WILLIAM T. BACON, Acting Ensign.

ROBERT BOYD, Midshipman January, 1850, Captain July 16, 1862, commanded a division of Miss. River Squadron 1864.

CHARLES H. BRADFORD, Corporal of Co. D, First Maine and 1st Lieut. of U. S. Marines, was taken prisoner at Fort Sumter, Sept. 7th, 1863, and died of wounds Feb. 15th, 1864.

HENRY A. BROWN, Acting Third Asst. Engineer, May 13th, 1864.

JOSEPH W. CHANDLER, Acting Ensign, Jan. 28, 1863.

CHARLES H. CHOATE, Acting Ensign, Jan. 8, 1863.

SAMUEL B. CLARK (father of Capt. Daniel C. Clark, killed in the Fifth Maine), served during the war as Acting Master. Dead.

GEORGE H. COLBY, Acting Ensign, Oct. 27, 1863.

CHALRES O. DAVIS, app. Acting Ensign, Dec. 9th, 1863.

WM. E. DENNISON, now Captain of the "City of Richmond," was a Volunteer Lieutenant, and had command the gunboat "Cherokee," in 1864.

EDWIN E. DRAKE, Acting Ensign; lost at sea by foundering of the brig "Bainbridge," August, 1863.

CHARLES H. HANSON, originally a "blue jacket." Acting Masters Mate, July 13th, 1863, promoted to Acting Ensign.

ARTHUR LIBBY, Acting Asst. Third Engineer, Jan. 9th, 1863.

WILLIAM G. MITCHELL, Acting Master, Nov. 2d, 1861.

ROBERT K. MORRISON, Acting Asst. Third Engineer, Oct. 17th, 1863.

JOHN W. NORTH, held commission as sailmaker during the war, and is now at home on the retired list.

HENRY M. NOYES, Acting Third Asst. Engineer.

EDWARD ERNEST PREBLE entered Navy in 1859, served through the war. Resigned about 1871 as Lieut.-Commander. Dead.

HENRY A. PROCTOR, Acting Master's Mate, May 31st, 1863.

HENRY O. PROCTOR, Acting Ensign, Aug. 13th, 1864.

HON. THOMAS B. REED, our distinguished Member of Congress, was an Acting Assistant Paymaster. He was light and supple then. What a miserable failure he would make of it now, trying to stand tip-toe on the main truck!

WENTWORTH P. RICHARDSON, Surgeon First Maine, Asst. Surgeon U. S. Navy, July 30th, 1861. Died July 20th, 1864.

JOHN SEARS, Acting Ensign, April 9th, 1863.

CHARLES B. STAPLES, Acting Ensign, Aug. 22d, 1862. Dead.

ROBERT B. SWIFT, Acting Third Asst. Engineer.

MARTIN W. THAXTER, Acting Third Asst. Engineer, May 31st, 1864.

WILLIAM E. THOMES, Acting Master.

N. BRADFORD WALKER, Acting Masters Mate, Aug. 27th, 1862. Dead.

JOHN D. WILLIAMS, Sergeant B, Twelfth Me., and Third Asst. Engineer; later Second Asst. Engineer U. S. Rev. Marine.

*EVERGREEN CEMETERY.

A	CO.	SEC.	NO. OF LOT.
Abbott, Clarence L.,	C, 32d,	E	18
Allen, Horace W.,	9th.		
Atwood, Hiram,	K, 17th.		

B

Bacon, Fred. A. G.,			
Bailey, David,	C, 17th.		
Baker, Chas. P.,	C, 29th,	F	
Barnard, J. E.,	A, 1st.		
Barbour, H. D.,	A, 9th,	E	37
Barker, N., Capt., Gen. Howard's staff, Q. M. dept.,		F	181
Batchelder, Granville,	A, 25th.		
Beal, G. W., Sergeant-Major,	24th,	F	91
Blakenburg, John.			
Blake, William.			
Blades, William C.,	I, 30th.		
Boody, George D.,	H, 25th,	F	364
Bolton, Ai, Corporal,	F, 25th.		
Bond, C. W., Corporal,	F, 30th,	F	10
Bonney, Edward M.,	C, 10th,	E	66
Bowen, H. A.			
Boyd, Parker Dwight, Captain,	U. S. A.		
Brackett. C. D.			
Brackett, C. E.,	F, 2d.		
Bragdon, C. W. M.,	E, 10th,	D	101
Breslin, Thos. H., Surgeon,		K	119
Broughton, Wm. H., Captain,	D, 16th.		
Brown, B. F.,	12th,	F	6
Brown, F. A.	G, Coast Guard.		
Brown, William A.,	A, 1st,	F	26
Brown, Charles L.,	C, 29th.	E	85

*Soldiers' Graves decorated Memorial Day, 1884. Please send notice of errors to Adjutant of Bosworth Post.

42   PORTLAND SOLDIERS AND SAILORS.

	CO.	SEC.	NO. OF LOT.
Budden, John jr., Corporal,	G, 13th,	F	95
Buckley, C. S.			
Burbank, George E.,	E, 17th,	F	
Burnell, Edward A.,	F, 29th,	D	86
Burnell, William,		J	55
Burnham, O. W., Lieutenant,	C, 17th,	M	54

C

Carter, Henry T.,	12th.		
Chandler, George.			
Chamberlain, George,	29th Unassig'd Co., C		72
Chadwell, George H., Captain,	H, 32d.		
Chase, W. F.,	5th Battery.		
Chase, Ruel D., Corporal,	F, 8th,	H	85
Clark, F. E.,	A, 25th,	E	183
Clark, Daniel C., Lieutenant,	G, 5th,	C	50
Clark, Samuel B.,	Navy,	C	50
Clough, Moses,	1st Battery,	J	164
Cole, J. W.,	F, 27th,	H	41
Cobb, George R.,	B, 17th.		
Cobb, Marston L.,	B, 10th,	F	360
Colby, Albert.			
Conant, Washington,		I	44
Corning, Clarence L., Captain,	17th, U. S. A.		
Crediford, C. H.,	E, 25th.		
Cross, A. P.,	E, 13th,	5	5
Cummings, Charles,	U. S. Navy.		
Cummings, Lucius H.,	G, 12th,	G	54
Cushman, Benjamin S.,	B, 10th,	K	44
Cushman, Charles H.,	B, 10th,	K	44
Cushman, H. H., Sergeant,	G, 1st,	F	112

D

Davis, E. W.,	A, 6th,	K	38
Davis, George H.,	G, 10th.		
Dodge, J. H.,	C, 31st.		
Downs, Joseph S.,	B, 10th.		
Downing, Sidney F.,	F, 11th,	N	482
Dyer, A. S., Lieutenant,	H, 5th.		

PORTLAND SOLDIERS AND SAILORS. 43

	E	CO.	SEC.	NO. OF LOT.
Edwards, John, Colonel,		U. S. A.		

F

Falby, J. C.,			F	152
Farmer, J. L.,			F	288
Fessenden, James D.,		Brig.-Gen. Vols.		
Fessenden, Menzies R., Capt.,		I, 12th.		
Fessenden, Samuel, Lieutenant,		Gen. Tower's Staff,	M	125
Fickett, George L.,		A. 25th,	N	68
Fitzgerald, John G.,		U. S. Navy,	F	191
Floyd, Charles R.,			E	34
Forsyth, J. A.,		G, 9th,	E	250
Frazier, J. A.,		12th.		
Furbush, Nehemiah T., Capt.,		F, 10th,	I	74
Furlong, A. W.,			H	74
Fuller, B. C.,		1st Battery,	F	

G

Gallison, G. W.,	A, 27th.			
Gardiner, W.,	6th,		E	224
Gerrish, E. Scott,	1st Battery,		F	416
Gerrish, W. L.,	7th Battery.			
Gilman, C. H., Captain,	G, 7th.			
Glenn, W. H.,	I, 29th.			
Goddard, John, Colonel,	1st Cavalry.			
Goldthwait, G. F., Corporal,	A, 31st.			
Gray, H. A., Lieutenant,	H, 9th.			
Green, J. W.,	H, 2d.			
Graffam, F. A.,	B, 10th.			
Gribben, Wesley, Corporal,	E, 13th.			
Grover, Almon,	E, 12th,		N	414
Grover, Alpheus,	F, 30th.			
Green, W. H.,	G, 29th,		J	67
Grant, A. K. P.,	D, 1st Heavy Art.			

H

Hall, William A.,	A, 25th,		F	
Hagan.				
Hamlin, L.				
Hanna, G. F.,	D, 17th,		E	241

44   PORTLAND SOLDIERS AND SAILORS.

	CO.	SEC.	NO. OF LOT.
Hanson, Warren,	B, 25th.		
Hanson, Charles H.			
Harward, William E.,	7th N. G. S. N. Y.,	N	349
Haynes, H. C., Sergeant,	4th Battery,	K	17
Headman, J. B.,		E	263
Hersom, N. A., Surgeon,	17th.		
Hinkley, O. D.			
Hinkley, O. W.			
Horr, Henry J.,	6th Battery,	I	90¼
Holmes, F. E., Sergeant,	F, 13th.		
Hudson, James O.,		E	62
Hudson, Josephus.			
Hyde, N.,		E	178
Hyde, R. W.,	A, 1st,	B	107

I

Ives, R. A.

J

Jackman, Woodbury L.,		N	601
Jones, F. L., Captain,	A, 25th.		
Jones, Merwin,		E	10
Johnson, F. T.,		D	

K

Kennard, C. O.,	5th Battery.		
Kimball, Bradford D.,	A, 25th,	E	17
Kimball, J. B.,	A, 19th,	F	29
Kimball, R. B.,		E	254
Knight, J. B.			
Knight, W. W., Hos. Steward,	29th,	F	21
Knight, J. K.			
Kennard, Frank S.,	A, 1st.		

L

Lake, Joseph F., Corporal,	A, 17th.		
Lang Charles F.,	K, 1st Cavalry,	N	167
Larrabee, C. F., Sergt.-Major,	30th,	E	222
Leavitt, G. W.,		E	181
Leavitt, J. W.,		E	179

PORTLAND SOLDIERS AND SAILORS. 45

	CO.	SEC.	NO. OF LOT.
Leslie, James W.,	D, 17th.		
Libby, Louis,	D, 20th.		
Littlefield, John.			
Little, C. F., Lieutenant,	B, 12th.		
Lowell, G. W., Corporal,	A, 25th,	M	151
Lyon, A. P.			
Littlefield, Charles,	H, 32d.		
Libby, C. H.			
Libby, D. S.,	D, 9th.		

M

	CO.	SEC.	NO. OF LOT.
Maxwell, J. H. N.,		D	101
Marston, S. M.			
McAllister, G. L.,	20th Unassig'd Co.,	E	143
McAllister, Charles L., Lieut.,	A, 1st,	J	62
McDuffee, C. E.			
Merrill, Charles E.			
Merrill, Ezra,		C	70
Merrill, S. H.			
Meserve, J. H..	E, 1st Cavalry.		
Morse, Charles F.,	E, 1st,	F	
Morse, Lorenzo D.,		D	78
Morse, Albert S.			
Moulton, George F.,	B, 17th,	N	375
Mountfort, D. E., Corporal,	B, 10th,	J	208
McLellan, Charles E., Corporal,	B, 12th,	F	250
M, no stone.			
Meserve, C. H., Captain,	D, 1st.		
Mathews, John,	F, 31st.		
Maynard, C. D.,	G, 29th,	M	156

N

	CO.	SEC.	NO. OF LOT.
Newman, A. P.,	1st Battery,	H	67
Newman, John,		H	67
Norwood, Chester,	A, 31st,	C	55
Noyes, George F.,		N	

P

Partridge, C. A.,	K, 1st Cavalry.	
Partridge, F. A.,	I, 1st Cavalry.	
Partridge, Joseph.		

46   PORTLAND SOLDIERS AND SAILORS.

	CO.	SEC.	NO. OF LOT.
Pennell, Benjamin C.,	B, 17th.		
Pearce, William A.,	D, 1st.		
Perry, D. O., Surgeon,	10th,	G	41
Perry, Joseph A., Captain,	F, 17th.		
Peyret, Henry,	K, 30th,	K	34
Phinney, Augustus,	E, 25th,	B	92
Preble, H. O.,		M	
Proctor, John.			
Plummer, H. A., Sergeant,	E, 29th.		
Paine, John S.,		M	99
Partington, J.,	H, 25th,	C	23
Proctor, John E., Sergeant,	G, 7th.		

R

Raymond, Augustus H.,		H	87
Records, L. L.,		F	
Remick, Josiah, Quartermaster,	17th,	M	101½
Roach, J. A. J.,	B, 9th,	M	50
Roberts, Edward A.,		N	
Roberts, James S.,	B, 17th.		
Roberts, J. H.,		C	44
Roberts, J. R. S.,	B, 17th,	B	33
Root, N. W. T., Chaplain,	Conn. Regiment,	N	569¼
Ross, G. H.,			
Russell, J. H., Lieutenant,	I, 1st D. C. Cav.		
Ross, J. G., Quarterm'r Sergt.	9th.		
Russell, Frank,	1st Vt. Cavalry.		
Rice, Joseph H.,	29th.		
Runnels, G. A.,	B, 31st.		
Randall Charles R.,		E	16

S

Sanford, D. W.,		G	39
Sawyer, Ellis M., Captain,	E, 17th.		
Shepley, Geo. F., Brig.-Gen., Col.,	12th,	M	7
Shaw, E.,		F	154
Sinclair, George H.,	K, 12th,	C	34
Stanley, J. H.			
Stanley, S. R.			
Stevens, C. B.,	G, 7th.		

PORTLAND SOLDIERS AND SAILORS. 47

	CO.	SEC.	NO. OF LOT.
Stevens, C. B.,	F, 1st Veterans,	F	119
Stevens, O. B.,		F	48
Stevens Jarvis T., Adjutant,	1st Cavalry.		
Stiles, S. G.,		J	187
Strong, George,	B, 12th,	J	
Strayton, G. E.			
Small, J. R.,		F	118
Snowman, Merrill,	D, 1st Battalion,	D	32
Somerby, J. P.,		K	49
Soule, F. E.,	F, 1st Veterans,	F	116
Soule, R. H.,	E, 29th,	F	116
Swett, John,	B, 10th.		
Shaw, Charles R., Sergeant,	A, 25th,		33
Stevens, D. H.,	H, 12th,	N	70
Stanley, S. H.,	K, 3d.		
Staples, Charles B., Captain,	U. S. Navy.		
Stoddard, W. P.,		J	171
Stubbs, C. R., Corporal,	6th Battery.		

T
Thaxter, Martin W.,	U. S. Navy,	H	
Thompson, George W.,		F	287
Thompson, Zenas, Chaplain,	6th,	F	
Thompson, J. S.,	1st D. C. Cavalry,	H	55
Todd, Charles R.,	A, 17th,	F	481
Trefethen, John M.,		E	178
Trowbridge, G. N.,		E	57
True Bros. (3),		G	78
Tukey, George W., Captain,	A, 1st,	E	68
Tukesbury, L. F.,	11th Mass.		

U
Unknown, 6.

V
Vanhorn, Charles F.,	E, 17th,	N	265

W
Walker, Adeline, Miss,	Hospital Nurse,	J	112
Walker, J. E., Captain,	D, 1st Veterans,	E	254
Walker, Nathaniel B.			

48   PORTLAND SOLDIERS AND SAILORS.

	CO.	SEC.	NO. OF LOT.
Walker, Thomas,	U. S. Navy.		
Wallace, C. H., Sergeant,	G, 1st Cavalry,	C	33
Wallace, C. E.			
Waterhouse, J. Thatcher, Q. M.,	17th,	M	46
Waterhouse, Samuel O.,	F, 13th,	G	37
Waterhouse, Peter B.,	B, 10th,	F	21
Waterhouse, Robert,	A, 17th.		
Webb, Charles D., Lieutenant,	A, 12th.		
Webber, A.,			
Wells, Charles C.,		G	31
Wescott, H. H., Corporal,	H, 25th,	J	
Wescott, R. T.,		E	41
Willis, Leonard.			
Winslow, Hiram,	B, C. G. H. Art.,	E	256
Witham, Albion, Lieut.-Col.	1st,	E	145
Whittier, George H.		J	197
Whitney, I. R., Sergeant,	F, 16th,		
Wallace, J. C. H.			

Y

York, James B.,	B. 1st,	N	653
Young, C. G., Musician,	5th,	C	30

*EASTERN CEMETERY.

A
Alden, Rear Admiral,   U. S. Navy.

B
Bradish, David, Major,   Revolution.
Briggs, John B., Doctor,   U. S. Navy.
Blythe, Captain,   English Brig "Boxer."
Blake, F. W. C.,   16th.
Burroughs, W. M., Commander,   U. S. N., "Enterprise."
Brown, John A., Sergeant,   5th Battery.

C
Cammett, George H.,   29th.
Cook, David, Captain,   Revolution.
Crossman, J. A.,   Revolution.

*Soldiers' graves decorated Memorial Day, 1884. Please send notice of errors to Adjutant of Bosworth Post.

D
Duran, George E. H.,   B, 17th.

G
Gill, Leonard F.,   13th.

H
Hoit.
Hunkins, Seth C., Surgeon,   4th.

K
Knight, Captain.

M
Mitchell, F. A.,   29th Mass.
Mitchell, J., Jr.
Montgomery, Thomas J., Captain,   U. S. Army.
Murch Charles R., Captain,   13th.

N
Nichols, Martin, Colonel,   Revolution.

O
Osgood, Francis, Brigadier-Gen.,   Revolution.

P
Pearson, Moses,   Revolution.
Plummer, S. M., Captain,   E, 9th.
Preble, Edward, Commodore,   U. S. Navy.
Preble, Edward E., Lieut. Comm'g,   U. S. Navy.

R
Reynolds, Thomas,   U. S. Navy.

S
Sheppard, Lewis,   Revolution.
Smith, John K., General,   Revolution.
Stanworth, John K.

W
Ward, Captain,   27th.
Wadsworth, Lieutenant,   U. S. Navy.
Water, Kervin, Lieutenant,   U. S. Navy.
Willard, Doctor.
Work, John,   C, 31st.

*WESTERN CEMETERY.

A
Allen, Robert, Jr.
Armstrong, Jacob,   A, 17th,
†Ayers, John, Captain,   A, 16th.
Alexander, Wm. H.,   C, 5th.
Alexander, Reuben, Lieutenant,   B, 10th.

B
†Burnham, James,   I, 15th.
Brissell, George F.
Bean, Wm. A. S.
Bradish, David.
Burnham, Henry A.,   C, 10th.
Bond, Edwin C.
Burr, W. H.,   G, 40th N. Y.
Bryan, Frank,   B, 17th.

C
Carruthers, Charles E.
†Clough, A. W., Captain,   H, 13th.
Chick, Amos.
Cole, Daniel, Sergeant,   E, 11th.
Courtland, C. W.
Cummings, Charles,   U. S. Navy.
†Cummings, Moses B.,   B, 1st Heavy Artillery.

D
†Deane, Wm. Wallace, Adjt.,   12th.
Densmore, Eben S.
Dinsmore, E. R.
Drake, James A.
Duncan, C. C.

G
Goold, Josiah,   E, 10th.
Gillispie, William.
†Green, John.
Gibby, George F.

H
Hamilton, Charles E.,   K, 1st Cavalry.
†Hamilton, Charles,   D, 19th.

*Soldiers' graves decorated Memorial Day, 1884. Please send notice of errors to Adjutant of Bosworth Post.
†No stone.

Hossack, Albert S.
Hardenbrook, Charles W.
Huntress, James, Corporal,   1st Battery.
Hurd, George,   H, 27th.
Hurd, William A.,   E, 15th.
Huff, Samuel, jr.

J
*Jackson, John B., Surgeon,   125th U. S. Col'd Troops.

L
Leggett, William.

M
McCann, Charles M.
Mason, D. W., Musician,   G, 5th.
McMasters, John,   C, 9th.
McKenney, Orin,   F, 5th.
Moses, Alfred L.,   B, 1st.
Milliken, George S.
Milliken, Frank, Lieutenant,   G, 26th.
Murphy, Edward,   G, 7th.

N
Nason, Elisha.
Newcomb, Abram,   D, 1st.
Noyes, Clarence W.

O
Osgood, George H.,   E, 20th.

P
Parsons, Joseph.
Pettingill, William.
Poor, Thomas H., Corporal,   D, 1st.
Prince, Henry.

R
Riggs, James.
Roberts, Lizzie Miss,   B. R. C.

S
Sawyer, A. H.,   H, 15th.
Sawyer, Wm. A.
Skillings, Franklin,   A, 17th.
Small, Clement P.,   1st D. C. Cavalry.
*Small, Moses,   F, 2d.

*No stone.

PORTLAND SOLDIERS AND SAILORS.

Small, Wm. B.,	G, 19th.
*Scott, Edward.	
Safford, Samuel D.,	A, 25th.

T

Ten Broeck, Herrick, Surgeon,	U. S. A.
Thompson, Joseph, Jr., Corp.,	E, 1st.
Trask, Charles H.,	B, 10th.
Trask, George.	
*Townsend, L. P.	

U

Unknown, 3.

W

Waterhouse, Edwin K.

†CALVARY CEMETERY.

A

| Anglin, William, | F, 13th. |

B

| Bingham, John A., | I, 12th. |
| Black, Thomas, | 1st Battery. |

C

Conroy, Francis.

| Crowley, Daniel, | D, 8th N. J. |

D

Daley, Peter,	G, 29th.
Daley, James,	H, 31st.
Deehan, Michael,	20th.
Devine, Anthony,	C, 20th.
Devine, Cornelius,	G, 1st Cavalry.
Devine, Thomas M.,	1st Battery.
Drouey, Timothy.	
Dolan, James.	
Dolan, Patrick.	

F

Fitzsimmons, John.
Flaherty, P. F.,	F, 13th.
Feeney, John,	1st U. S. Artillery.
Fox, Thomas,	H, 20th.

*No stone.
†Soldiers' graves decorated Memorial Day, 1884. Please send notice of errors to Adjutant of Bosworth Post.

H
Hennesey, Daniel,   C, 30th.
Hoffman, Frank.

J
Jackson, Robert,   B, 7th.

K
Kaler, William M.
Kelley Patrick.

L
Landers, James,   E, Heavy Artillery.
Lee, Edward,   C, 61 Mass.

M
Manning, James,   G, 1st.
Manning Michael,   D, 1st.
McCarty, John,   U. S. Navy.
McCarty, Timothy,   1st Battery.
McQuinn, Henry A.,   1st Battery.
McMain, Edward,   U. S. Navy.
McMain, Thomas,   U. S. Navy.
McGuire, Patrick,   A, 14th.
McFarland, George,   C, 86th N. Y.
Megee, Thomas,   D, 17th.
Megee, M. C.,   A, 10th U. S. A.
Maloney, Patrick.
McGrath, Patrick,   A, 17th.
Mathews, James,   1st Battery.

O
O'Brion, Timothy,   29th.

S
Scaulan, Peter,   U. S. Navy.
Sheehan, John,   F, 29th.
Sheehan, John,   I, 30th.
Smith, Michael,   15th.
Sheridan, James,   C, 10th.
Spellman, Jeremiah,   F, 20th.
Stokes, Thomas,   I, 2d.

T
Tobin, Patrick,   17th U. S. A.
Tobin, William.
Tracy, William,   I, 30th.

W

Walsh, Thomas,	D, 19th.
Wharton, Joseph,	K, 12th.

U

Unknown, 36.

*FOREST CITY CEMETERY,
CAPE ELIZABETH.

A

Armstrong, George L.,	9th.
Annis, John,	6th Battery.
Ayer, Llewellyn,	C, 14th.

B

Bourness, J. I. C.,	K, 15th.

C

Coolbroth, Asbury,	F, 6th.
Cottrell, M. J.	
Call, Nathan,	H, 27th.
Clawson, Fred.	

D

Dow, Jedediah.	
Dyer, Elisha,	I, 25th.

E

Elliott, John G.,	E, 1st Cavalry.

F

Fogg, Isabella Miss,	Hospital Nurse.
Fields, Edmund D.,	D, 17th.

H

Haskell, Edward C.,	H, 25th.

J

Jones, Calvin,	D, 7th.
Jones, Medbury.	

K

Kimball, Augustus A.,	B, 17th.

L

Lown, John E.,	F, 30th.
Litchfield, John.	

*Soldiers' graves decorated Memorial Day, 1884. Please send notice of errors to Adjutant of Bosworth Post.

PORTLAND SOLDIERS AND SAILORS.

M
Murphy, Jeremiah,   I, 2d.

O
O'Brion, Patrick.

P
Palmer, J. F.,   H, 13th.

R
Rose, James,   U. S. Navy.

S
Sawyer, C. M.,   E, 8th.
Stinson, Alexander,   J, 20th.
St. John, William W.

W
Williams, Augustus,   B, 9th.
Wyman, A. A.

---

*BROWN'S HILL CEMETERY,
CAPE ELIZABETH.

C
Cash, Charles E.,   C, 12th.
Clark, J.

H
Hutchinson, William A.

L
Libby, Samuel C.

S
Skillin, William H.,   G, 13th.

---

*MOUNT PLEASANT CEMETERY,
Meeting House Hill, Cape Elizabeth.

B
Burbank, Edward.
Burbank, Israel.

*Soldiers' graves decorated Memorial Day, 1884. Please send notice of errors to Adjutant of Bosworth Post.

PORTLAND SOLDIERS AND SAILORS.

D
Downs, Nahum,	E, 19th.
Dyer, William H.,	E, 12th.

E
Eneast, Henry.

G
Gibson, Robert,	C, 29th.
Gilbert, James M.,	E, 29th.
Graffam, George H.,	B, 30th.
Graffam, Joshua P.,	I, 25th.
Gurney, James.	

H
Hartman, Charles,	G, 5th.

J
Jordan, Andrew,	G, 1st Cavalry.
Jordan, James W.,	U. S. Navy.
Jordan, Oliver.	

L
Lincoln, Robert.	
Leavitt, James 2d,	5th Battery.

M
Miller Henry P., Corporal,	I, 25th.

N
Nickerson, William.

P
Payne, Robert.

R
Richardson, Wm. H.

S
Skillins, Stephen.

W
Webster, John L. S.,	I, 25th.
Walden, Green, Capt.,	U. S. R. M.
Woodbury, Joseph H.,	I, 25th.

Two reported as soldiers buried in paupers' graves were decorated. Three "unknown" graves in Western Cemetery, six in Evergreen, fifty-six in Forest City, and four in Mt. Pleasant were decorated on account of flags that were found over them. The flags have been renewed from year to year, because the graves were originally pointed out to previous committees as soldiers' graves.

www.ingramcontent.com/pod-product-compliance
Lightning Source LLC
Chambersburg PA
CBHW061515040426
42450CB00008B/1623